Fact Finders®

CAUSE AND EFFECT: AMERICAN INDIAN HISTORY

Seeking Freedom

CAUSES AND EFFECTS of the Flight of the Nez Perce

BY HEATHER E. SCHWARTZ

Consultant:
Brett Barker, PhD
Associate Professor of History
University of Wisconsin–Marathon County

CAPSTONE PRESS
a capstone imprint

Fact Finders Books are published by Capstone Press,
1710 Roe Crest Drive, North Mankato, Minnesota 56003
www.capstonepub.com

Library of Congress Cataloging-in-Publication Data
Schwartz, Heather E.
Seeking freedom : causes and effects of the flight of the Nez Perce / by Heather E. Schwartz.
  pages cm.—(Fact finders. Cause and effect: American Indian history)
  Summary: "Explains the flight of the Nez Perce, including its chronology, causes, and lasting effects"—Provided by publisher.
  Includes bibliographical references and index.
  ISBN 978-1-4914-2034-8 (library binding)
  ISBN 978-1-4914-2209-0 (paperback)
  ISBN 978-1-4914-2224-3 (ebook PDF)
1. Nez Perce Indians—Relocation—Juvenile literature. 2. Nez Perce Indians—Government relations—Juvenile literature. 3. Joseph, Nez Perce Chief, 1840–1904—Juvenile literature. 4. Nez Perce Indians—Wars, 1877—Juvenile literature. I. Title.
  E99.N5S39 2015
  979.5004'974124—dc23   2014037519

Editorial Credits
Catherine Neitge, editor; Bobbie Nuytten, designer; Eric Gohl, media researcher; Morgan Walters, production specialist

Source Note
Page 23, line 1: *Harper's Weekly*, vol. 21, #1090, 17 Nov. 1877, p. 906. "The Surrender of Joseph." American Indians of the Pacific Northwest Collection. University of Washington. 18 Sept. 2014. https://content.lib.washington.edu/aipnw/surrenderofjoseph.html

Photo Credits
Alamy: North Wind Picture Archives, 19; AP Photo: *Lewiston Tribune*/Kyle Mills, 28; Art Resource, N.Y.: Washington State Historical Society, 7; Bridgeman Images: © Look and Learn/Private Collection, cover, 5, 20–21; Corbis: Christie's Images, 13; Getty Images: Nativestock, 11, Stock Montage, 9; Library of Congress: 12, 27; Newscom: Picture History, 22, Rob Crandall Stock Connection Worldwide, 29; Northwest Museum of Arts & Culture: Eastern Washington State Historical Society, Spokane, Washington/L94-7.105, 15; U.S. Forest Service: Nez Perce National Historic Trail, 17; Wikimedia: Washington State History Museum, 25

Design Elements: Shutterstock

Printed in Canada.
102014   008478FRS15

Table of Contents

Forced
FROM THEIR HOME

The Wallowa Mountains of Oregon had been the tribal homelands of the Nez Perce for more than 10,000 years. In the late 1800s, the U.S. government ordered them out. Five **bands** that had refused to leave had just 30 days to gather supplies and move to an Idaho **reservation**. If they didn't go, they'd be forced out by the U.S. Army.

Tribal leaders decided they should leave the Pacific Northwest peacefully and try to meet the July 1877 deadline. Members of the tribe were angry, however. At a campsite a few young warriors took revenge for earlier wrongs. They killed some white settlers, sparking the U.S. military into action.

About 750 Nez Perce men, women, and children headed east, with soldiers in hot pursuit. During the next three months, they traveled more than 1,000 miles (1,609 kilometers) through Idaho, Wyoming, and Montana. Many lost their lives trying to hold off the army while they made their escape.

Less than 40 miles (64 km) away from safety in Canada, the Nez Perce lost their last battle. Forced to surrender, their flight ended in a crushing defeat for the tribe.

Chief Joseph and other tribal leaders led the Nez Perce on a desperate flight for freedom.

band—group of related people who live and hunt together

reservation—an area of land set aside by the government for American Indians; in Canada reservations are called reserves

What Caused
THE FLIGHT OF THE NEZ PERCE?

In 1800 Nez Perce territory stretched across 17 million acres (6.9 million hectares) in Washington, Montana, Oregon, and Idaho. Members of the tribe traveled according to the seasons to hunt and fish.

Today Nez Perce territory consists of about 770,000 acres (311,608 hectares) on the Nez Perce Indian Reservation in northern Idaho. Why did the Nez Perce, who call themselves the Nimiipuu, leave their land?

Cause #1: The Treaty of 1855

By the mid-1800s white settlers had started moving into Nez Perce territory. In the settlers' eyes, white American **culture** was better than American Indian culture. They thought it was their God-given right to take over the land. They believed in an idea called **Manifest Destiny**.

The U.S. government struck a deal with the Nez Perce in 1855. If the tribe would give up some land, the government would allow them to keep the rest. Their remaining territory would become a reservation for the Nez Perce. They would have the right to decide who could live there.

An 1855 watercolor features the Nez Perce arriving to sign the treaty.

With no other options, the Nez Perce signed the **Treaty** of 1855. They lost close to 7.5 million acres (3 million hectares) of tribal land to the United States. But they kept their ancestral home in the Wallowa Valley of northeastern Oregon.

culture—a people's way of life, ideas, art, customs, and traditions
Manifest Destiny—the belief that God gave white Americans the right to take over North American land that belonged to other people
treaty—an official agreement between two or more groups or countries

Cause #2: Discovery of Gold

The Treaty of 1855 didn't protect the Nez Perce for long. In 1860 gold was discovered on the Nez Perce Reservation. Miners went after the gold even though they didn't have a legal right to be on the land.

The miners set up camps. They even established the town of Lewiston, Idaho. The Nez Perce were being crowded out of their own territory. Yet they couldn't stop the white settlers from coming in.

The Nez Perce had the Treaty of 1855 on their side. Now they needed the government to step in and defend their rights. They believed it was time to expel the illegal settlers from the Nez Perce Reservation. Instead, the U.S. government looked the other way. When government leaders finally took action, officials ignored the treaty they'd signed with the Nez Perce. They disregarded the Nez Perce's rights.

An 1863 poster advertised steamboat passage to western gold fields.

HO FOR THE YELLOW STONE

AND  THE

GOLD MINES
OF IDAHO!

A NEW AND VERY LIGHT DRAUGHT STEAMER WILL LEAVE

SAINT LOUIS FOR BIGHORN CITY!

THE JUNCTION OF BIGHORN AND YELLOW STONE RIVERS,

SATURDAY, APRIL 2D, AT 12 O'CLOCK M.

Parties taking this route save 400 miles river transportation and over 100 miles land transportation. Bighorn City being by a good wagon road from Virginia City 200 and from Bannack City 205 miles.

I WILL ALSO SEND TWO LIGHT DRAUGHT SIDE-WHEEL STEAMERS

TO FORT BENTON

One leaving at the same time, and the second about fifteen days later. I am prepared to contract for Freight and Passage either to Bighorn City or Fort Benton.

refer to W. B. DANCE, JAS. STEWART and N. WALL, Virginia City, or to M. MANDEVILLE, Bannack City.

For Freight or Passage apply to **JOHN G. COPELIN,**

Care JOHN J. ROE & CO., St. Louis, Mo

Cause #3: The Treaty of 1863

By law the U.S. government should have forced the white settlers to leave Nez Perce territory. But the growing country's leaders broke the law. They didn't want to remove settlers from the valuable land. Instead, they struck another deal with the Nez Perce. The Treaty of 1863 took 7 million more acres (2.8 million hectares) of their land, including the Wallowa Valley. It became known as the "steal treaty."

The treaty was signed, but not all bands of the Nez Perce agreed. Some felt they had no choice. They hoped the U.S. government would help the tribe gain needed resources if they signed. Others refused to sign the treaty and give up their land. U.S. leaders decided that one band of Nez Perce could sign an agreement for the entire tribe. That wasn't what many Nez Perce believed. The resistance by five bands marked the start of the conflict that would lead to the 1877 flight.

If some Nez Perce refused to go quietly, the U.S. government decided that it would have to find a way to make them leave.

A Brief Victory

The U.S. government made an effort in 1873 to help Nez Perce who wanted to stay on their land. White settlers in half of Oregon's Wallowa Valley were ordered to leave the territory to the Nez Perce. The U.S. reversed its position in 1875, however, and took back the order.

The Wallowa Valley in Oregon

Cause #4: Forced Removal

The U.S. decided in 1877 that even Nez Perce bands that did not sign the treaty must obey it. Leaders from both sides met. But the nontreaty Nez Perce couldn't be convinced to leave their homeland in Oregon and move to less desirable land in Idaho. U.S. Army General Oliver Howard was in charge of enforcing the Treaty of 1863. He gave the Nez Perce a choice. They could arrive at the Lapwai reservation in Idaho within 30 days, or the army would attack them.

The deadline gave the Nez Perce little time to prepare. They would have to leave before the Snake and Salmon rivers fell to a safe level for crossing. Still, they didn't have much of a choice. The Nez Perce leaders who had resisted the move decided to lead their people to the reservation. They were chiefs Joseph, White Bird, Looking Glass, Husishusis Kute, and Toohoolhoolzote. It seemed the only way keep the peace.

General Oliver Howard

Chief Joseph

The great Nez Perce leader who became known as Chief Joseph was born in northeastern Oregon in 1840. His name translated as Thunder Rolling Down from the Mountain. He was the son of a chief, also named Joseph. His father believed there could be peace between the Nez Perce and the U.S. government. But the elder Joseph felt betrayed by the Treaty of 1863. When he died in 1871, his son Joseph took over as the tribe's leader.

Chief Joseph in 1903.

Cause #5: Nez Perce Anger

The Nez Perce were leaving, but they weren't happy about the decision. A group of young warriors felt especially angry. They didn't believe they should have to give up their homeland in Oregon. Some felt personally wronged by white settlers. They wanted revenge for their relatives who had died at the hands of whites.

In June 1877 the Nez Perce were at what is now called Tolo Lake, near their reservation in Idaho. The young warriors decided to avenge their relatives' deaths.

Naming Tolo Lake

Tolo Lake is named after a Nez Perce woman, Tulekats Chikchamit. She was often called "Tule" for short and whites misunderstood it as "Tolo." She saved lives by warning white settlers in Florence, Idaho, of an attack. Whites rewarded her by making her the only Nez Perce permitted to claim a piece of land outside the reservation.

The warriors attacked and killed 17 settlers. Communities of settlers panicked. The Nez Perce panicked too. Most of them didn't want trouble. There was no chance for peace with the United States now.

Knowing the army would soon come after them, the Nez Perce began their difficult journey. The flight of the Nez Perce was also the start of the Nez Perce War.

Chiefs Joseph, White Bird, and Looking Glass are in the front and center of the Nez Perce band.

THE
Flight

The flight of the Nez Perce was far from peaceful. It was marked by a series of brutal battles with the army.

The first battle took place at Idaho's White Bird Canyon on June 17. The Nez Perce had fled there to prepare for **retaliation** by the army. Soldiers and volunteer **civilians** headed there to make arrests for the attack and arrange a **truce**. But as they approached, a volunteer fired at the Nez Perce. The Nez Perce quickly fired back. The U.S. forces retreated, but not before 34 soldiers were killed. Once again, the Nez Perce fled.

retaliation—attack in response to a similar attack
civilian—a person who is not in the military
truce—an agreement to stop fighting in a war

The Flight of the Nez Perce

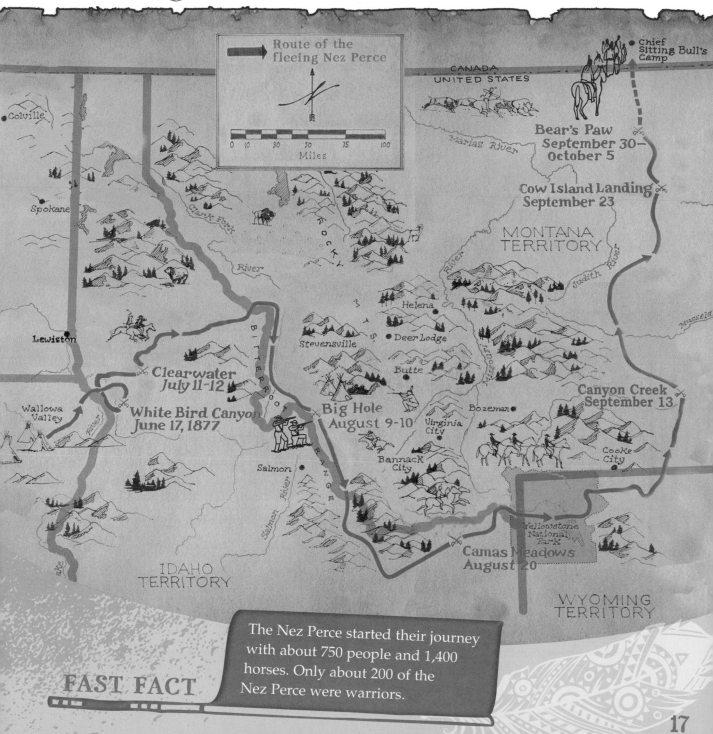

Route of the fleeing Nez Perce

0 10   30   50   75   100
Miles

CANADA
UNITED STATES

Chief Sitting Bull's Camp

Bear's Paw
September 30–October 5

Marias River

Cow Island Landing
September 23

MONTANA TERRITORY

Judith River

Mussels

Colville

Spokane

Clark Fork

River

ROCKY

Helena

Lewiston

Stevensville

Deer Lodge

Butte

Canyon Creek
September 13

Clearwater
July 11-12

BITTERROOT

White Bird Canyon
June 17, 1877

Big Hole
August 9-10

Bozeman

Virginia City

Cooke City

Wallowa Valley

River

RANGE

Bannack City

Salmon

Salmon River

Camas Meadows
August 20

Yellowstone National Park

IDAHO TERRITORY

ake

WYOMING TERRITORY

FAST FACT

The Nez Perce started their journey with about 750 people and 1,400 horses. Only about 200 of the Nez Perce were warriors.

The Battle at Big Hole

The army caught up with the Nez Perce at the Clearwater River in Idaho on July 10. After two days of fighting, the army took over the Nez Perce camp. From there, the Nez Perce fled toward Montana. They hoped to convince their friends, the Crow, to join the fight and help them.

But the Crow did not want to join the war. The Nez Perce set up camp at Big Hole Basin, believing they'd outrun the army and were safe in Montana. They planned to rest, then head toward safety in Canada. They hoped to join Lakota leader Chief Sitting Bull. He had also fled to Canada after the Battle of the Little Bighorn the previous summer.

While the Nez Perce were sleeping, however, U.S. Army Colonel John Gibbon led a surprise attack on them. Fierce fighting on August 9 cost 89 Nez Perce and 31 soldiers and volunteers their lives. Most of the Nez Perce killed weren't warriors engaged in the battle. They were women and children.

The Nez Perce who survived had to move quickly. If they could make it across the border to Canada, they would escape to safety.

General Howard's soldiers chased the Nez Perce for months.

Camas Meadows and Canyon Creek

From Big Hole the Nez Perce traveled back into Idaho and then to Yellowstone National Park in Wyoming. General Howard was on their trail. To slow him down, some Nez Perce warriors raided Howard's camp on August 20. They meant to steal and scatter his horses, but more fighting broke out.

The Nez Perce traveled through Montana, hoping to reach safety in Canada.

FAST FACT

Yellowstone National Park was established as the country's first national park in 1872. That meant the U.S. government owned the land and would protect it from overdevelopment.

The Nez Perce continued their flight to Canyon Creek, Montana, where U.S. Colonel Samuel Sturgis led the next attack on September 13. Nez Perce warriors fought them off, buying time for women, children, and elderly members of the tribe to escape. The Nez Perce suffered, however, when the Crow took up the army's side. The Crow helped the army steal Nez Perce horses. Now the Nez Perce would have a much more difficult time trying to outpace the soldiers.

Final Battle

By the time the Nez Perce reached the Bear Paw Mountains in Montana, they were exhausted. Supplies were running out. They had been fighting and fleeing for months. On September 30 another battle with the army began.

After five days of fighting, the Nez Perce knew they couldn't win and they couldn't continue. U.S. military leaders were impressed the Nez Perce had lasted so long. Chief Joseph had earned the nickname "the Red Napoleon." His skills and tactics were equal to those of Napoleon Bonaparte, leader of France in the early 1800s. Nevertheless, the Nez Perce War ended October 5, 1877, with Chief Joseph's surrender.

Frederic Remington painted Chief Joseph's surrender in the late 1880s, about 10 years after the event.

"I am tired of fighting," said Joseph. *"Our chiefs are killed. … It is cold, and we have no blankets; the little children are freezing to death. My people, some of them, have run away to the hills, and have no blankets, no food. No one knows where they are— perhaps freezing to death. I want to have time to look for my children, and see how many of them I can find. Maybe I shall find them among the dead.*

"Hear me my chiefs! I am tired; my heart is sick and sad. From where the sun now stands I will fight no more forever."

After the surrender about 230 Nez Perce escaped into Canada. The rest—87 men, 184 women, and 147 children—were moved to a reservation. They'd traveled 1,170 miles (1,883 km) since leaving their homeland. They were less than 40 miles (64 km) from safety in Canada.

FAST FACT

Throughout their flight through the mountains the Nez Perce warriors fought against more than 2,000 U.S. soldiers.

What Effects Did the FLIGHT OF THE NEZ PERCE HAVE?

The Nez Perce War was one of the last major conflicts between American Indians and the United States. When Chief Joseph surrendered, U.S. leaders gained the upper hand. They were free to move the Nez Perce as they saw fit.

Effect #1: End of the Conflict

Chief Joseph negotiated an agreement that his band of Nez Perce would be taken to the Lapwai reservation in Idaho. But U.S. leaders decided to move them to Kansas and then to a reservation in Indian Territory instead. The winter journey was difficult. The Nez Perce were transported in unheated railroad cars, and three children died along the way. Once they reached the reservation in present-day Oklahoma, many more people died of disease. About eight years later, the Nez Perce were moved again, this time to reservations in Washington and Idaho.

Chief Joseph continued to negotiate with the U.S. government and worked tirelessly to help his tribe. But he was never allowed to return to his beloved Wallowa Valley. When Chief Joseph died in 1904, his doctor said it was from a broken heart.

Chief Joseph and his family
at Fort Leavenworth, Kansas.
They were being sent to a
reservation in Indian Territory.

25

Effect #2: Growth of U.S., Loss of Traditions

After the war the United States grew stronger while the Nez Perce lost almost everything. They lost the power to determine where—and how—they lived. With the Nez Perce out of the way, the United States continued to expand. Settlers could now freely move onto former Nez Perce lands in Washington, Montana, Idaho, and Oregon. Confined to reservations, the Nez Perce could no longer travel throughout the large territory to hunt and gather food according to the seasons.

After the Nez Perce were forced off their land, their culture remained under attack. The United States Indian Training and Industrial School was established in 1879. It was the first of many **boarding schools** opened for American Indian children. At the schools the next generation of American Indians was forced to turn away from their native culture. Boys had to cut their traditional long hair. Students were not allowed to wear native clothes or use their Indian names. They were not allowed to speak their native languages.

boarding school—school where students live

American Indian children were forced to attend boarding schools far from their homes. They rarely saw their families.

Effect #3: Nez Perce Grew Stronger

Despite the odds, and although the United States won the Nez Perce War, the tribe eventually regained its power. Students who had been educated at boarding schools did not lose their culture forever. Many used what they'd learned to become tribal leaders.

Today there are about 3,500 members in the Nez Perce tribe. More than half of them live on the Lapwai reservation in northern Idaho.

Modern Nez Perce run programs to manage their land and natural resources. The tribe's fisheries program was established in the early 1980s to restore shrinking fish populations and habitats. The Nez Perce Horse Registry was established in 1995. Its goal is to bring back the tribe's horse culture and breed the Nez Perce horse.

The Nez Perce horse breed is gentle and smart. The horses enjoy being around people.

Cause and Effect

The flight of the Nez Perce drove them away from their beloved homeland. This allowed the United States to grow. But the expansion came at a great cost to the Nez Perce.

Tepee poles mark the site of the 1877 Nez Perce camp at the Big Hole National Battlefield.

GLOSSARY

band (BAND)—group of related people who live and hunt together

boarding school (BOR-ding SKOOL)—school where students live

civilian (si-VIL-yuhn)—a person who is not in the military

culture (KUHL-chuhr)—a people's way of life, ideas, art, customs, and traditions

Manifest Destiny (MAN-uh-fest DESS-tuh-nee)—the belief that God gave white Americans the right to take over North American land that belonged to other people

reservation (rez-er-VAY-shuhn)—an area of land set aside by the government for American Indians; in Canada reservations are called reserves

retaliation (ri-tal-ee-AYE-shuhn)—attack in response to a similar attack

treaty (TREE-tee)—an official agreement between two or more groups or countries

truce (TROOS)—an agreement to stop fighting in a war

READ MORE

Biskup, Agnieszka. *Thunder Rolling Down the Mountain: The Story of Chief Joseph and the Nez Perce*. American Graphic. Mankato, Minn.: Capstone Press, 2011.

Dwyer, Helen, and Mary A. Stout. *Nez Perce History and Culture*. Native American Library. New York: Gareth Stevens Pub., 2012.

Rice, Earle, Jr. *The Nez Perce of the Pacific Northwest*. We Were Here First: The Native Americans. Kennett Square, Pa.: Purple Toad Publishing., 2013.

INTERNET SITES

FactHound offers a safe, fun way to find Internet sites related to this book. All of the sites on FactHound have been researched by our staff.

Here's all you do:

Visit *www.facthound.com*

Type in this code: 9781491420348

Super-cool stuff! Check out projects, games and lots more at **www.capstonekids.com**

CRITICAL THINKING USING THE COMMON CORE

1. In 1872 the U.S. government established Yellowstone National Park to protect the land. Why do you think the government was willing to protect parks, but unwilling to protect American Indian land? (Key Ideas and Details)

2. The Nez Perce were peaceful people. Yet they battled the United States throughout their flight. Do you think they had any other options? (Integration of Knowledge and Ideas)

3. After the Nez Perce War, U.S. military leaders said they were impressed with the Nez Perce and Chief Joseph. What could they have done differently so their actions matched their words? (Integration of Knowledge and Ideas)

INDEX